You Can Have an EPIC Marriage!

Drs. Bob & Donna "LOVE"

The "LOVE" Couple

DEDICATION & ACKNOWLEDGMENTS

Dedication, acknowledgments, credits and thanks to our Lord and Savior, Jesus Christ, our EPIC marriage that God has so graciously blessed us with, our seven children, the Holy Bible and to the World Wide Web (definitions, etc).

CONTENTS

Introduction

Marriage is a covenant! Marriage is a mirror image of our relationship with our Lord and Savior, Jesus Christ. Marriages should reflect Him. Marriage should be a reflection of Christ and His bride, us. When we look in the mirror, as a couple, do we see Jesus Christ? Do we display Christ to our spouses, to our children, to our family, to our friends, and to the world? Are we leaving a legacy for our children to duplicate what is modeled for them?

We have been married for almost 25 years and we have enjoyed this journey every step of the way. Our marriage is definitely EPIC!!! Praise the LORD!!! We're not called the "Love Couple" for nothing! ☺ We have seven children and three of our children are young adults, who are excited about the idea of having a marriage and family of their own!

Marriage takes work! It is a job! Since, it's a job, consider all that you do to exemplify Christ on your job. Be encouraged to fight for your marriage and to do whatever it takes to leave a lasting legacy for generations to come!

This short read will encourage you to reflect Christ in some practical ways. You will discover how to be an "EXCELLENT" wife and a husband of "VALOR". We have implemented these tools and pray that in some form, it will encourage you to do the same. You can choose to use this book as a couple devotion, as a couple small group Bible study, or just read it alone. However, you decide to use this book, we pray that your marriage will be forever changed and that you will leave a legacy of an "EPIC MARRIAGE" for generations to come!!!

Mark 10:8-9

AND THE TWO SHALL BECOME ONE FLESH; so they are no longer two, but one flesh. "What therefore God has joined together let no man separate."

How to become a MIGHTY MAN of VALOR?

And the angel of the LORD appeared unto him, and said unto him, The LORD *is* with thee, thou mighty man of valor. -Judges 6:12

What is a man of valor? Valor means having great courage in the mist of danger. Valor is the qualities of a hero; exceptional or heroic courage when facing danger (especially in battle). A man of valor means being brave and having a strength of mind in regard to danger; that quality which enables a man to encounter danger with firmness; personal bravery; courage; prowess; intrepidity.

How can we be godly husbands in an ungodly world?

The Bible gives us **eight requirements** of a godly husband. **HUSBAND** is the "house-band," connecting and keeping together the whole family. As we meet the basic requirement of a godly husband we will meet our wives basic needs.

1. The first *requirement* of a godly husband is to **<u>submit</u>** to his wife. **Eph. 5:21** "Submitting yourselves one to another in the fear of God."
    a. **Value** is a basic need for a wife. Submitting to your wife means valuing her opinion. Two opinions is/are always better than one.

    b. Submitting to your wife means listening to her. It doesn't mean you will always agree with her but you definitely listen to her. James 1:19 says "let every man be swift to hear, slow to speak, slow to wrath".

2. The second *requirement* of a godly husbands is to **lead** his wife- **Ephesians 5.23** For the husband is the head of the wife, even as Christ is the head of the church: and he is the savior of the body. **1 Corinthian. 11.3** But I would have you know, that the head of every man is Christ; and the head of the woman is the man; and the head of Christ is God.

   a. **Partnership** is a basic need for the wife. Wives want their husband's participation in raising the kids, making decision around the house, leading in spiritual things. They want you to do life with them, not live two separate lives in the same household.

   b. God is head of Christ, Christ is head of man and man is the head of woman. The husband is the head of the wife.

3. The third *requirement* of a godly husband is to **love** his wife. **Ephesians 5.25-33**; Colossians 3.19 says, "love and be not bitter against them". We are called to love her more than our jobs, cars, hobbies, mom, kids, family and friends.

Two Expressions of Love:

   a. **Love** is a basic need for a wife. The first expression is to love your wife as Christ loves the church v. 25. The word "love" is agape which means seeking the highest good for another person (unconditional love). This is an unselfish love as seen in Christ sacrificial death in which He gave Himself up for the church. How do you love her as Christ love the church? The text gives us *three examples* on how to love our wives as Christ loves the church?

      i. The first example on how to love your wife like Christ is to practice giving _v.25 **"Husbands, love your wives, even as Christ also loved the church, and *GAVE***

himself for it" (John 3:16). You can't love without giving. *You give your wife money-she gives you a meal, you give her a house-she gives you a home, you give her seed-she gives you a baby,*. The nature of man is to give and the nature of woman is to receive. "I give myself away, so you can use me"

ii. The second example on how to love your wife like Christ is to <u>promote the Word</u> v. 26, **"That he might sanctify and cleanse it with the washing of water by the *WORD*"**

- The Word will <u>sanctify</u> her meaning it will <u>set her apart</u>. Is your wife set apart from your mom, daughter and every other female? You can speak words to your wife, you can't speak to no other female (intimate words, sacred/sanctified/sexual words)

- The Word will <u>cleanse</u> her.. meaning it will <u>set her free</u> from defilement, faults and sin. When you speak the Word over your wife it will evoke her beauty and bring the best out of her.

iii. The final example on how to love your wife like Christ is to <u>present her without blemish</u> (not having spot or wrinkle) v 27 "**That he might present it to himself a glorious church, not having spot, or wrinkle, or any such thing; but that it should be holy and without blemish.**"

b. The second expression is to **love your wife as you love yourself.** How do you love her as yourself? Ephesians 5:28-33 gives us **5 ways** to love your wife as you love yourself.

a. The first way is to **Protect** her (Nourish) –the word nourish in the text means to bring up, to care for (v. 29a). How have you protected your wife recently? We are called to protect our wives. We should protect her physically, emotionally and spiritually. In John 15.13, it proclaims that "Greater love hath no man than this, that a man lay down his life for his friends". A husband should be willing to lay down his life for his wife. Are you willing to protect your wife?

b. The second way is to **Prize** her-(Cherish)- The word cherish means to foster, warm in one's bosom (v. 29b). Prize means to be given as a reward to the winner. Your wife is the winner of your heart! A lot of other men were in the competition, but you won her heart. When you put that ring on her finger, that told her that she was your most prized possession on this earth. Your wife is your trophy, so display her for the world to see. The greatest gift you can give your kids is to prize their mother. Your wife is your most prized possession. Have you prized your wife?

c. The third way is to **Prioritize** her: One must be willing to leave his father and mother (v. 31a). Prioritize means to designate or treat as more important than other thing. Your wife should come before your mother, father, boss, kids, and friends. Your wife comes before every human being on this earth. Have you prioritized your wife?

d. The fourth way is to **Pursue** her. One must be joined unto his wife (v. 31b). Pursue means to follow in order to catch. Men pursue your wives daily. The same charm you used to get her, is the same charm it will take to keep her. Keep pursuing your wife, there is a lot you can still learn about her. Are you pursing your wife?

    e. The final way is to **Partner** with her. The two shall be one flesh (v. 31c). Your wife is the best partner you can have. A partner can see things you can't see, hear things you can't hear, and do things you can't do. A partner has your best interest at heart! Your spouse should have your back at all times and you should always have her back, too! We have to be willing to accept their constructive criticism and correction. Always remember your wife is not your competitor, but your companion. Have you partnered with your wife today?

4. The fourth *requirement* of a godly husband is to **live joyfully** with his wife. Ecclesiastes 9:9 says "Live joyfully with the wife whom thou lovest all the days of the life of thy vanity, which he hath given thee under the sun, all the days of thy vanity: for that is thy portion in this life, and in thy labour which thou takest under the sun."

    a. **Attention** is a basic need for wife. Wives want to be listened to and know that we believe what they have to say is important.

    b. Men are to truly listen to what your wife is saying. We listen not only with our ears, but we listen with our eyes, too. Give that woman eye contact. Giving her eye contact is giving her your undivided attention.

    c. The only way we can live joyfully with our wives is to have the right priorities. The word joy is a great acronym for having the right priorities in your live.

J- - Jesus should be first in our lives.

O- others should be second in our lives.

Y- you should be last in your life.

When we have the right priorities we will experience joy. The joy of the Lord is our strength.

5. The fifth *requirement* of a godly husband is to **learn to honor** his wife - 1 Peter 3.7 says, "Likewise, ye husbands, dwell with them according to knowledge, giving honour unto the wife, as unto the weaker vessel, and as being heirs together of the grace of life; that your prayers be not hindered."

   a. **Romance** is a basic need for wife. One easy way to honor your wife is to **romance** her. Wives want a little romance in the marriage such as notes, flowers, candy, surprises, hotel, message, bubble bath, and cleaning up the house.

   b. Honoring your wife is respecting your wife. It is easy for us to honor our mother, boss and friends. But it is difficult for us to honor our wife. Men we are to dwell with her, honor her and pray for her.

6. The sixth *requirement* of a godly husband is to **labor to provide** for his wife. 1 Timothy 5.8 says, "But if any provide not for his own, and especially for those of his own house, he hath denied the faith, and is worse than an infidel."

   a. **Protection** is a basic need for wife. Provide **protection** for your wife. Wives want their husbands to be the defender of the family; not just against sounds in the night, but against all the threats in society. You should provide protection for your wife.

   b. Your wife wants you to take ownership in leading the family spiritually. In other word initiate prayer and bible study in the home. Don't leave your families spiritual growth to a preacher on Sunday morning. Provide spiritual stability in your family.

   c. Men are you providing physically, emotionally and spiritually protection for your family?

7. The seventh *requirement* of a godly husband is to be **loyal** to his wife Read Proverbs. 5:15-20. Loyalty means being faithful and dependable. Loyalty promotes security. Security is one of the major needs of a wife.

   a. **Security** is a basic need for wife. The wife wants to know you are going to be there forever. When your wife is secure you will be satisfied (mentally, physically and spiritually).

   b. Rejoice with the wife v.18

   c. Ravished (go astray, intoxication) with your wife v. 19. Proverbs 5:15-20 says "Drink waters out of thine own cistern, and running waters out of thine own well. [16] Let thy fountains be dispersed abroad, and rivers of waters in the streets. [17] Let them be only thine own, and not strangers' with thee.[18] Let thy fountain be blessed: and rejoice with the wife of thy youth. [19] Let her be as the loving hind and pleasant roe; let her breasts satisfy thee at all times; and be thou ravished always with her love. [20] And why wilt thou, my son, be ravished with a strange woman, and embrace the bosom of a stranger?"

8. The final *requirement* of a godly husband is not to sexually deprive his wife. **Intimacy** is a basic need for a wife. For a woman intimacy doesn't always mean sex, it can mean touching, hugging, communication and/or kissing. She wants to know that she is on your mind constantly!

When do you abstain from sex? 1 Corinthians 7:1-5
Here is a list of reasons to abstain from sexual intimacy.

   a. Except mutual consent (agreement) of time

   b. Except prayer

c. Except fasting

The scripture says nothing about a headache. I know of a married couple who have not had sex in two years. That is dysfunctional, ungodly and lead to affairs. Your body doesn't belong to you, it belongs to God and your spouse.

What is the purpose of sex? There are **four purposes for sex.**

1. The first purpose of sex is for **procreation:**

   a. Genesis 1:28 says, "And God blessed them; and God said to them, 'Be fruitful and multiply, and fill the earth, and subdue it; and rule over the fish of the sea and over the birds of the sky, and over every living thing that moves on the earth.'"

   b. God doesn't give us children just so that we can have a look a likes. He give us children so that His image can be transferred.

2. The second purpose of sex is for **pleasure:** Prov. 5:19 Let her be as the loving hind and pleasant roe; let her breasts satisfy thee at all times; and be thou ravished always with her love.

   a. Heb. 13.4 Marriage *is* honourable in all, and the bed undefiled: but whoremongers and adulterers God will judge.
   b. Song 1:2, "May he kiss me with the kisses of his mouth! For your love is better than wine."
   c. Song 2:3, "Like an apple tree among the trees of the forest, so is my beloved among the young men. In his shade I took great delight and sat down, and his fruit was sweet to my taste."
   d. Song 4:6 Awake, O north wind; and come, thou south; blow upon my garden that the spices thereof

may flow out. Let my beloved come into his garden, and eat his pleasant fruits.

3. The third purpose of sex is for **prevention of fornication and adultery**: 1 Corinthians 7: 1-5 says, "Now concerning the things whereof ye wrote unto me: It is good for a man not to touch a woman. [2] Nevertheless, to avoid fornication, let every man have his own wife, and let every woman have her own husband. [3] Let the husband render unto the wife due benevolence: and likewise also the wife unto the husband. [4] The wife hath not power of her own body, but the husband: and likewise also the husband hath not power of his own body, but the wife. [5] Defraud ye not one the other, except it be with consent for a time, that ye may give yourselves to fasting and prayer; and come together again, that Satan tempt you not for your incontinency". The word defraud means to take something from someone by means of deception or trickery.

4. The fourth purpose of sex is for a **purity covenant**

   – Men were circumcised as a sign of covenant. Read Genesis 17.10-12.

   – The consummation of the marriage was a woman's convent with her husband. Read Deuteronomy 22.13-15.

   – Your Sexual organs bear the mark of the covenant!

How does God view sex?

- Sex is God's idea
- Sex is a gift from God
- Sex is a spiritual issue
- Sex is a legitimate passion given by God
- Sex brings oneness

How to become a WOMAN OF VIRTUE?

What does **virtue mean**…. Having moral excellence; characterized by morality; upright; righteous; pure; as, a virtuous action.

It is choosing to have right standards, strength, courage, modesty, and purity… all done in EXCELLENCE. We acquire virtue by our faith, our obedience to Christ, being persistent in Him, and clothing ourselves in Him.

The Scripture we'll be coming from is Prov. 12:4.

<u>King James Bible</u>
A **virtuous woman** *is* a crown to her husband: but she that maketh ashamed *is* as rottenness in his bones.

<u>New American Standard Bible</u>
An **excellent wife** is the crown of her husband, But she who **shames** him is like rottenness in his bones.

How are we a crown to our husbands and how can we KEEP him happy??? YES, we are crowns to our husbands! I am a crown to my husband, POOH!

In other words, a wife can bring the greatest joy to her husband or the greatest misery. When we look at the crown and what it represents, we see the crown is a public item that glorifies its wearer. The crown is a sign of rule. The crown is also a symbol of strength and power. This is what the writer is alluding to, in the above Scripture. Basically, an excellent wife defines a man's strength, power, and authority. Wives we carry great power with our husbands. When he is confident in us, we become his crown. He stands taller. He feels he can conquer the world, because we got his back! A virtuous woman rules by the power of her love and the graces of her life. An excellent wife is a crown, because she brings immediate glory to her husband. He is proud to be seen with her and to call her his own. Now, the opposite of being his crown, we can choose to bring him shame, which is like a rottenness in his bones, a disease that weakens him from the inside. Such a wife poisons her husband's life, deprives him of strength and life; though she is made "bone of his bones, and flesh of his flesh" (Genesis 2:23), far from being a helpmate for him, she drains his very existence.

However, whatever a man does, wherever he goes, his wife should make him look REAL good! I have some tools that I will share, that has been successful in being the CROWN to my husband. Ladies, we want to bring dignity and honor to the man of God that HE has blessed us with.

I want us to learn how to be a VIRTOUS/EXCELLENT wife and bring honor to our husbands by making our husbands CROWN brightly shine and ultimately reflect CHRIST!

We can be virtuous women and be the crown to our husband by yielding to Christ and fulfilling these **four requirements**.

The 1ˢᵗ Requirement is to LOVE GOD PASSIONATELY!

Luke 10:27 [27] And he answering said, Thou shalt love the Lord thy God with all thy heart, and with all thy soul, and with all thy strength, and with all thy mind; and thy neighbour as thyself.

Our spiritually growth w/Christ is vital in marriage, not only for the growth of our marriages, but also, as an example for our children to see and duplicate. When we TRULY love God, it will reflect in our actions toward Him and everyone else around us. It is God's requirement that we love HIM! As a wife, we should follow hard after HIM…passionately. Passionately means, as a wife, we must spend quality time with Him daily. Daily prayer. When we **set the**

tone in the home…Set an atmosphere of worship…God's Presence is in our home. We must strategically pray for our husbands on a daily basis. Not only does prayer change our husbands, but it changes us at the same time. Daily devotion and reading/studying His Word is also important! Meditate and memorize Scripture.

In our home I strategically pray daily and play worship music to set the atmosphere of honor to our Lord! I also, have a prayer room that is set aside specifically to strategically to pray. I have a prayer wall and list of individuals I pray for and see God manifest Himself through.

Ladies we can create a happy home. Seeking the Lord and putting HIM first only increases our relationship w/the Lord, our spouse, and our family! We must make the Lord a priority.

Our 2nd Requirement as a wife is to LOVE OUR HUSBANDS PASSIONATELY.

Titus 2:4

[4] That they may teach the young women to be sober, to love their husbands, to love their children,

What does it mean to love our husbands?

The Bible describes 4 kinds of Love: 1. Storge: Affection, 2. Philia: Friendship, 3. Eros: Romance, and 4. Agape: Unconditional Love. All Christians are called to generally love, but wives are specifically called to love their husbands. The kind of love that God calls wives to isn't conditional and based upon feelings. This kind of love isn't the kind that you can "fall out" of. It isn't an optional love, *it's a commandment.* "Godly love is not primarily a feeling, it is a CHOICE. **LOVE IS A DECISION!!!**

In marriage, love is a WILLING of SELFLESSNESS for the good of someone else that <u>does not require reciprocation</u> or that the person being loved is <u>deserving</u>.

Love is based off of 3 principles:

- Love is demonstrating SACRIFICIAL action towards our husband.

  1. When we sacrifice for our husbands, it means keeping our husbands in focus as our **top priority**, over anyone else....other than Christ! Jesus is #1!

  2. When we sacrifice for our husbands, it means we should **serve him** when we don't feel like it. Serve him by cooking, cleaning, caring for the children, etc.

  3. When we sacrifice for our husbands, it means we make ourselves **available** for our husbands whenever he needs us, even when we don't feel like it.

- **Love is demonstrating an attitude** of unconditional acceptance.

1. We should accept our **husband as he is**. This acceptance should not be based on his performance, but on his worth as God's gift to you.

2. We should make sure value our husband's **thoughts and feelings**.

3. It's equally important to **accept him, despite his failures**. True love grants our husbands the freedom to fail, allowing the Holy Spirit to work in his life. When we look back at our own failures, this makes it easier for us to accept our husband's failures, as well!

- Love is **responding to your husband's physical needs. We'll call this the Marriage Act.**

What is the "MARRIAGE ACT"? Sex is the Marriage Act. We call it the "marriage act", because this is the ONLY WAY that Christ wants us to enjoy sex, according to the Scriptures! I will expand a little more about this from a wives perspective, because this is the big one...sexual intimacy. So many wives struggle with this in their marriage and many husbands and wives feel less than satisfied in their sex life. "The marriage act bond between husband and wife is a gift from God for the enjoyment of physical intimacy and the procreation of life. All that God created is good, and physical intimacy is no exception". God created sexual intimacy within marriage, and He created it as gift for us. But some wives can struggle to see this as a gift and only as an obligation instead. The bottom line is that God does intend for each couple **to have a sex life that is fulfilling for both husband *and* wife**. Scripture says in 1 Cor. 7:2-5, "Let each man have his own wife, and let each woman have her own husband. Let the husband fulfill his duty to his wife, and *likewise also the wife to her husband.* The wife does not have authority over her own body, but the husband does; and likewise also the husband does not have authority over his own body, but the wife does. Stop depriving one another, except by agreement for a time that you may devote yourselves to prayer". Therefore, our husband has freedom to enjoy our bodies (SONG 7:1-9) and we have the freedom to enjoy our husband's body (SONG 5:10-16), as well!

The marriage act can be improved **by BUILDING 4 areas**.

1. **COMPANINIONSHIP**: Companionship is nurtured through ROMANCE (sharing mutual interest...we love to work out together, do ministry together, AND dating on a regular basis). Companionship is also nurtured through TENDERNESS (this means affection and non-sexual touch)....AND THROUGH COMMUNICATION.
2. **COMMITMENT**: which is nurtured through BEING FAITHFUL (this includes developing a healthy attitude toward our husbands and toward sex intimacy in general AND FORGIVING our husband.
3. **CLOSENESS (SPIRITUAL INTIMACY):** this may seem a little strange, but trust us, it is an awesome way to

honor God and our husbands…praying before the marriage act is a great way to bring the presence of God in the bedroom and in our marriage. When we unite together spiritually first, it's as if our souls are drawn closer together. And when our souls are drawn together, we want to draw together in a deeper way. Prayer helps bring us into the "HOLY" Place! Additionally, praying and studying the word of God together creates a bond that is unexplainable! Remember, the marriage act is how we **express our oneness** in the covenant we made to one another!

4. **CRAVING (PASSION)**: PASSION is fired through **planning** (which means planning, making the marriage act a priority and scheduling it in the best part of our day), **unselfishness** (means I am committed to fulfilling HIS Needs, because **I am the only one** who can) **and creativity**(this means I want to **enhance the setting** and vary in our approach…).

Lastly, 1 Corinthians 13:4-7 basically sums up how we should love our husbands. We can do a self-examination of our love towards our husbands, based on this Scripture….and ask ourselves: Does this describe my love for my husband?

- Love never gives up.
- Love cares more for others than for self.
- Love doesn't want what it doesn't have.
- Love doesn't strut,
- Doesn't have a swelled head,
- Doesn't force itself on others,
- Isn't always "me first,"
- Doesn't fly off the handle,
- Doesn't keep score of the sins of others,
- Doesn't revel when others grovel,
- Takes pleasure in the flowering of truth,
- Puts up with anything,
- Trusts God always,
- Always looks for the best,
- Never looks back,

- But keeps going to the end (The Message).

As we love our husbands **sacrificially, unconditional acceptance, and with physical responding to his needs,** he can't help but notice us loving him as God does. And that is the kind of love that 1 Corinthians 13:8 says "*never* fails." **8** Love never fails. But where there are prophecies, they will cease; where there are tongues, they will be stilled; where there is knowledge, it will pass away. Additionally, we want to provide you with a Christian link that will help you answer some difficult question…you can write this down. http://site.themarriagebed.com/start-here .

Our 3rd Requirement as a wife is to LEARN TO SUPPORT OUR HUSBANDS.

Ephesians 5:22-23

22 Wives, submit yourselves unto your own husbands, as unto the Lord.

23 For the husband is the head of the wife, even as Christ is the head of the church: and he is the saviour of the body.

24 Therefore as the church is subject unto Christ, so let the wives be to their own husbands in **everything**.

The verb "submit" in the Greek is the word hupotasso, which is a military term which means to be ranked under in military order. This ranking of the wife under the husband's authority was sovereignly chosen by God, so that there will be order and harmony in the home. We, as wives have a different ranking or POSITION in the home. We're not an inferior person or a doormat, however. But we must recognize God's rankings of leadership in our home and that our husbands are the head…they are the leaders and we should support them, as such. Support is a choice to follow our husband's leadership. God created the husband to be the leader in marriage and the wife to be **his supporter/helper and completer** in marriage. (Gen 2:18) My husband sometimes calls me the voice of the Holy Spirit and that's because the HOLY SPIRIT is our helper, too!

When we support our husbands **we empower him** to be all that God intended him to be. **SUPPORT IS A CHOICE!!!** We must decide to support our husbands, so that we can HELP them reach their God given potential. When there needs are met, our needs are met, too!!!

Our support involves being:

*SUBMISSIVE

1. Submission is following our husband's leadership, even when we don't feel like it.
2. Submission is complementing our husbands and is not being competitive with our husbands. It is important to realize that we are on the same team.
3. Submission is cooperating with our husbands, as he seeks to lead our marriage and family through the guidance of the Holy Spirit.
4. Submission is demonstrating our support in our **1)** attitudes (*attitude of TRUST and *FAITH/*as a supportive wife we trust our husbands to make decisions even if they are sometimes wrong and *trusting that God can correct and change our husbands…we can't change our husbands.), **2)** IN our WORDS (some words that show we support our husband's leadership are *words of belief *words of help *words of affirmation), and our actions (*we should be ready to follow him where God leads him in his job, etc. *we must resist the temptation to be critical of our husband, even if his decision is not what we would have chosen for our family.)

*__PRAYERFUL__- WE SHOULD PRAY **STRATEGICALLY** FOR OUR HUSBANDS ON A DAILY BASIS and then trust God to answer our requests.

This is a great website link to guide us for strategically praying for our husbands on a daily basis.

https://www.reviveourhearts.com/articles/31-days-of-praying-for-your-husband/

It is important that we pray specifically….

- Pray for our attitude toward your husband to be more like Christ.
- Pray for his well-being, wisdom, protection, blessings, guidance, knowledge, spiritual maturity, success, purity, strength in temptation, etc.
- Look for God's answers to your prayers.
- Thank God for working in you and in him.
- Thank God for your husband.

Our 4th Requirement as a wife is to LIVE RESPECTFULLY WITH OUR HUSBANDS.

Ephesians 5:33b

33 and the wife see that she reverence her husband. **KJV**

33 and let the wife see that she respects and reverences her husband that she notices him, regards him, honors him, prefers him, venerates, and esteems him; and that she defers to him, praises him, and loves and admires him exceedingly. **Amplified**

Respecting our husbands is not an option, but a command from God. The Greek word for respect is phobeo which comes from a word that means "to be frightened or to be alarmed." It means to be in awe of, to revere, to reverence, or to treat as someone special." It is important to evaluate ourselves to see if we are respecting our husbands. When I was preparing for this particular topic, reverencing and respecting, I was tested and did an evaluation on myself and found that there were some areas that I still needed to work on. Respecting our husbands means we should continuously CHOOSE to respect our husbands. But what if we feel that he doesn't deserve our respect? Or what if it's "that time of month" and we just don't want to be bothered? Am I released from God's command? The answer is NO! This is not an easy topic, because our society says differently. Our society says women have their rights and can choose to do as they please. Unfortunately, that spirit has creeped into the church! However, it is our responsibility, as virtuous women and excellent women, to choose to respect our husbands as the LORD requires us to!

When we respect our husbands it means to **freely** regard our husbands with honor, reverence, and esteem. Respecting also involves us encouraging our husbands regularly, because this helps build confidence in them. Additionally, we should never criticize or correct our husband in public or in front of the children. When we encourage our husbands, we say and do things that **build him up**. Encouragement says, "I BELIEVE IN YOU! Respecting involves us admiring our husbands, because this energizes him. It is important to say, "I'm proud of you, honey!" Respecting our husband is understanding and appreciating our husbands, as well. We need to understand and appreciate the mass of our husband's responsibilities as the leader of our homes and appreciate his unique needs as a man.

When we, as women of virtue, treat our husbands as royalty kings and high priest of our homes, we are going to reap the benefits physically and spiritually! We must follow the commandments of the LORD and not the world!

Final Thoughts:

God wants us to have an EPIC marriage, but we have to do our part as mighty men of valor. We should submit to our wives, lead our wives, love our wives, live joyfully with our wives, learn to honor our wives, labor to provide for our wives, be loyal to our wives and sexually fulfill our wives.   I believe we have to fulfill these eight requirements of a godly husband, in order to have an EPIC marriage. The greatest gift you can give the world is to love your wife!

Furthermore, as we commit ourselves to God's way for marriage, then we will demonstrate what it means to be woman of virtue. We will be able to make evident the love, support, and respect our husband needs to become the servant-leader God has called him to be. Remember, God has designed a husband and wife to fulfill their responsibilities through dependence upon His Spirit and His Word.

Additional Resources by Drs. Bob & Donna "LOVE":

Order our first eBook on Amazon for only $2.99.

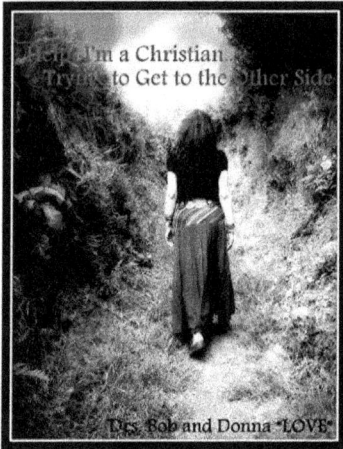

Order our first book on sale now for $4.99, plus shipping. Send an email to global.family.network.services@gmail.com.

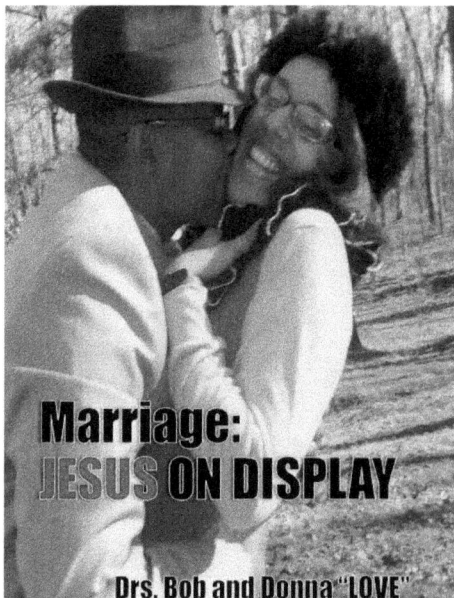

www.ingramcontent.com/pod-product-compliance
Lightning Source LLC
Chambersburg PA
CBHW071809020426
42331CB00008B/2451